Abington Public Library
Abington, MA 02351

P9-DNN-558

3 1627 01040 3486

Scribbles noted
6 - 17 AB. JB

$28.44
Bud

JACOB

ABINGTON PUBLIC LIBRARY
600 Gliniewicz Way
Abington, MA 02351

MACHINES ★ AT WORK

STREET SWEEPERS

BY E. S. BUDD

THE CHILD'S WORLD® • MANKATO, MINNESOTA

The Child's World

Published in the United States of America by The Child's World®
1980 Lookout Drive • Mankato, MN 56003-1705
800-599-READ • www.childsworld.com

PHOTO CREDITS
© Alvey & Towers Picture Library/Alamy: 4, 7
© David M. Budd Photography: 12, 16 (both), 19
© D. Hurst/Alamy: 8
© Gari Wyn Williams/Alamy: 11
© iStockphoto.com/Jill Fromer: 3
© Kitt Cooper-Smith/Alamy: 15
© Michael Klinec/Alamy: 20
© Richard Levine/Alamy: cover, 2

ACKNOWLEDGMENTS
The Child's World®: Mary Berendes, Publishing Director;
Katherine Stevenson, Editor

The Design Lab: Design and Page Production

LIBRARY OF CONGRESS CATALOGING-IN-PUBLICATION DATA
Budd, E. S.
  Street sweepers / by E. S. Budd.
    p. cm. — (Machines at work)
  Includes bibliographical references and index.
  ISBN 978-1-59296-952-4 (library bound: alk. paper)
  1. Street cleaning—Equipment and supplies 2. Street cleaning— Juvenile literature.
  3. Trucks—Juvenile literature. I. Title. II. Series.
  TD860.B77 2007
  628.4'6—dc22   2007013405

Copyright © 2008 by The Child's World®
All rights reserved. No part of this book may be reproduced or utilized in any
form or by any means without written permission from the publisher.

 **Contents**

This street sweeper is cleaning a street in England.

What are street sweepers?

Street sweepers are special machines. They sweep places clean. Roads and city streets get dirty. So do parking lots. Street sweepers clean these areas quickly. They keep our neighborhoods clean.

How are street sweepers used?

Streets get full of trash and dust. In snowy areas, they get full of salt and sand. This dirt gets into the air. That is bad for people's health. It also goes down drains and into rivers. That makes the water dirty. Street sweepers clean up the dirt instead.

This street sweeper keeps sidewalks and other small areas clean.

Larger street sweepers have two steering wheels. The driver uses the wheel on the side of the street being cleaned.

★ How do street sweepers work?

The driver sits in the **cab**. The cab has **controls**. The controls run the street sweeper. The sweeper has mirrors. They help the driver see all around. The driver moves the sweeper along slowly.

Many street sweepers have brushes on the sides. They let the sweeper clean a wider area. The brushes turn around and around. They act like brooms. They sweep dirt and trash under the machine.

This brush is on the side of the machine. It cleans the edge of the street. You can see how quickly it turns!

This street sweeper has a big brush on the back.

Abington Public Library
Abington, MA 02351

 Many sweepers have a bigger brush, too. It brushes up dirt from a wide area. It sweeps the dirt onto a **conveyor belt**. This belt carries the dirt into a bin.

Some street sweepers do not have conveyer belts. Instead, a **vacuum** sucks dirt into the bin. These machines are like giant vacuum cleaners.

Hose

This street sweeper has a vacuum. It also has a big hose on the back. The hose helps the driver clean hard-to-reach areas.

The big photo shows a driver filling the tank. The small photo shows how water sprays onto dusty streets.

 Roads often get dusty. Some sweepers spray water. It wets the dirt and dust. These sweepers carry a tank full of water. The driver fills the tank at a **fire hydrant**.

What happens when the bin is full?

The sweeper's bin fills up fast. Then the sweeper goes to the dump. Or it meets a truck that can carry trash. The bin raises up. It dumps out the dirt and trash. Now the sweeper can clean another street.

This sweeper is emptying its bin.

This street sweeper is cleaning up after a parade in Germany.

Are street sweepers important?

Street sweepers keep our streets clean. They clean up trash and dirt. They help keep people healthy. They help keep rivers clean. Street sweepers are very important!

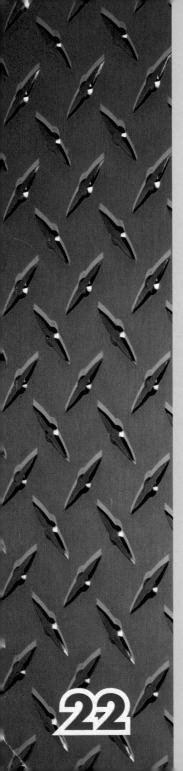

Glossary

cab (KAB) A machine's cab is the area where the driver sits.

controls (kun-TROLZ) Controls are parts that people use to run a machine.

conveyor belt (kun-VAY-ur BELT) A conveyor belt is a moving belt that carries things from place to place.

fire hydrant (FIRE HY-drunt) A fire hydrant is an outdoor pipe that provides water for fire trucks and other uses.

vacuum (VA-kyoom) A vacuum sucks up air, carrying dirt along with it.

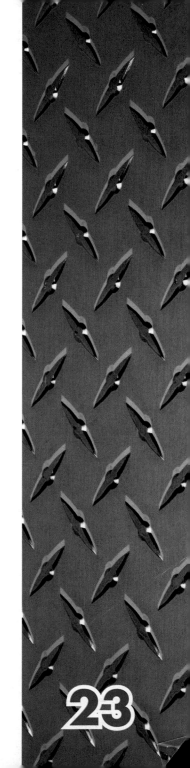

 Books

Bridges, Sarah, and Amy Bailey Muehlenhardt (illustrator). *I Drive a Street Sweeper.* Minneapolis, MN: Picture Window Books, 2006.

Moore, Patrick H. *The Mighty Street Sweeper.* New York: Henry Holt, 2006.

Sycamore, Beth, and Lee Macleod (illustrator). *Sweep!* New York: Little Simon, 2003.

 Web Sites

Visit our Web page for lots of links about street sweepers:
http://www.childsworld.com/links
Note to parents, teachers, and librarians: We routinely check our Web links to make sure they're safe, active sites—so encourage your readers to check them out!

Index

About the Author

E. S. Budd has written over fifty books for children, on everything from famous people and history to machines. She is married to David Budd, a photographer who took some of the pictures for this book. The Budds live in Colorado.